ALIEN

FACTS

#9

BY ZEESHAN MAHMUD

A steam powered mono-plane which had a test flight in 1898

TETRIS WAS THE FIRST VIDEO GAME EVER PLAYED IN SPACE!

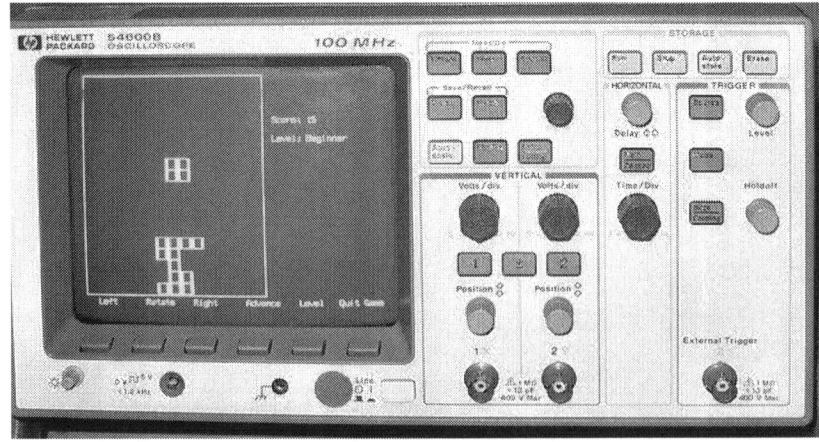

Al Qazwini Cosmology

"God created an angel who took [the earth] on his shoulders, and grasped it with his hands; the angel had as his support a rectangular rock of green hyacinth, itself borne upon a giant bull which rests upon a fish swimming in the water" (paraphrase of Qazwini i, 146, by Streck)

In the early 1900s, the "dropping a stone into a pool" sketch was the primary visual metaphor used to explain the "craze" of wireless telegraphy to a bewildered public. This popular educational illustration featured a man dropping a pebble into still water to show how invisible electromagnetic waves—pioneered by Guglielmo Marconi—radiated outward through the "ether" just like physical ripples. During this era, the concept of sending messages without physical wires was so revolutionary it was often viewed with a mix of scientific awe and "ludicrous" skepticism; newspapers used these sketches to demystify how a signal from a spark-gap transmitter could be "caught" by a distant antenna. This simple ripple analogy remains the foundational way we visualize everything from Wi-Fi to cellular networks, tracing its roots directly back to that turn-of-the-century telegraph mania.

A bizarre but major cultural obsession tied to the 1920s telegraph craze was "Spirit Telegraphy," a belief that wireless technology could bridge the gap between the living and the dead. Because early wireless signals were invisible and seemed to "pull voices from the ether," many

people, including prestigious scientists like Sir Oliver Lodge, viewed the technology as a scientific validation of spiritualism. This obsession peaked between 1917 and 1922, during which even Guglielmo Marconi and Nikola Tesla publicly claimed they were receiving strange, rhythmic signals—possibly in Morse code—that they believed might be attempts by Martians or extraterrestrial intelligences to communicate with Earth. This "ludicrous" intersection of high-tech radio and the occult led to the marketing of "spirit telephones" and "spirit trumpets," as well as a massive surge in Ouija board popularity, which newspapers at the time famously dubbed a "spiritual telegraph" for the masses.

The first experiments in driverless cars were conducted in the 1920s using radio control. In 1925, Houdina Radio Control demonstrated a radio-controlled "American Wonder" car through the streets of New York City, operated by a person in a trailing car.

In the early 1920s, the "Golden Age of Aviation" fueled a flurry of outrageous flying car concepts that blended whimsical science fiction with experimental engineering. A standout of this era was the 1921 Helica Leyat, a bizarre "car-airplane" prototype featuring a massive front-mounted propeller and a lightweight, plywood body designed to be steered like a plane on the road. This decade also birthed the wildly ambitious Pitts Sky Car in 1924, a vertical-lift machine equipped with a massive circular rotor of sixty hinged blades that, rather than achieving flight, famously only managed to bounce erratically on the ground. These early years were defined by such "ludicrous" attempts, where inventors like Hugo Gernsback envisioned gyroscopically stabilized "Helicars" with push-button controls to solve New York City's growing traffic congestion, setting a precedent for the century-long struggle to merge the garage with the hangar.

NES Tetris falling speed by level

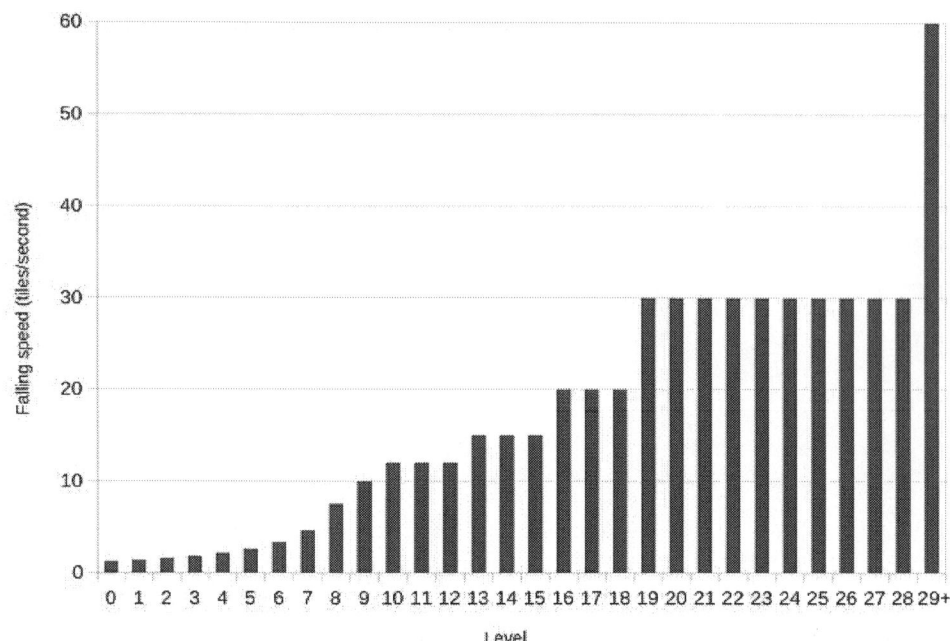

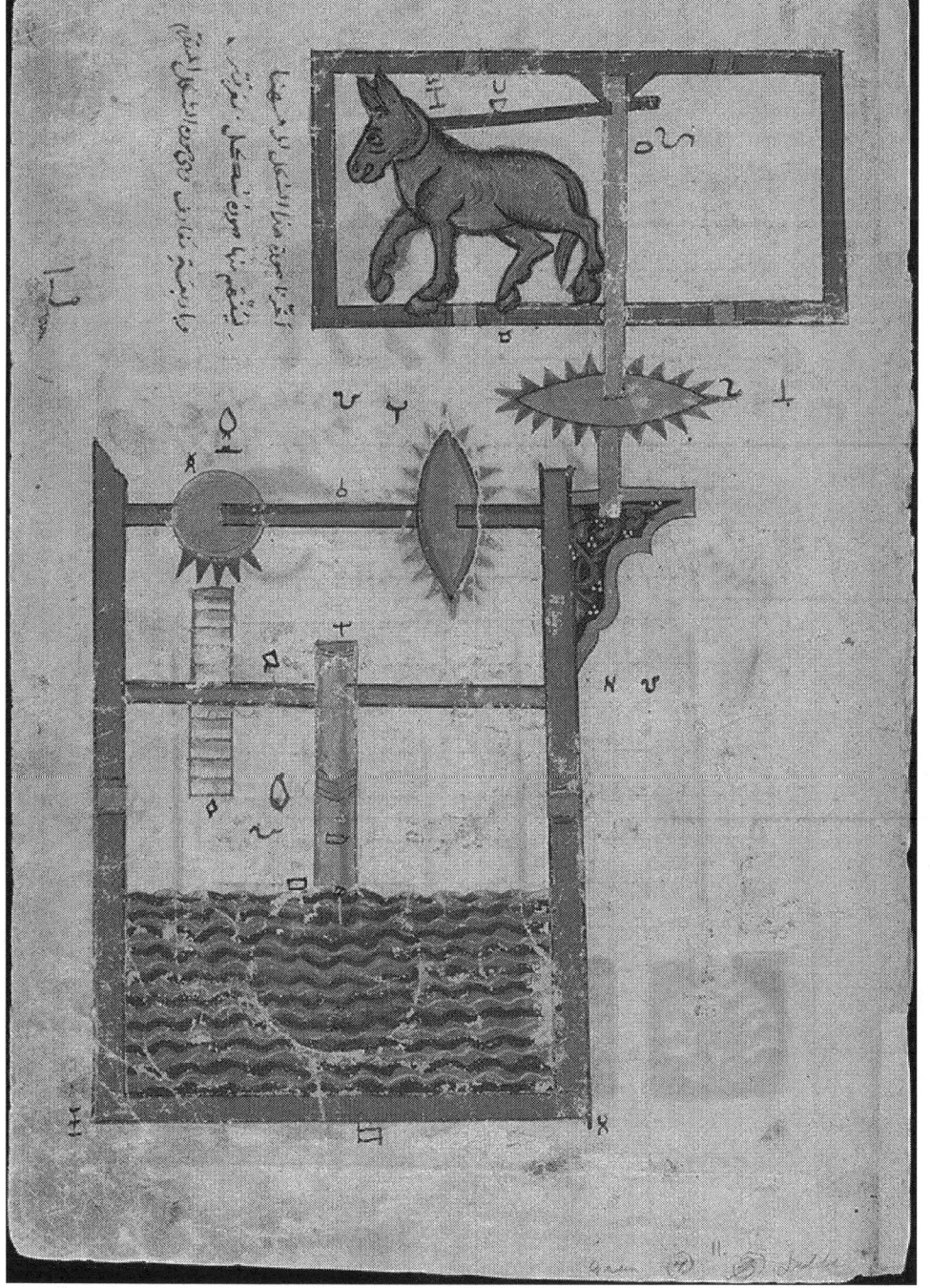

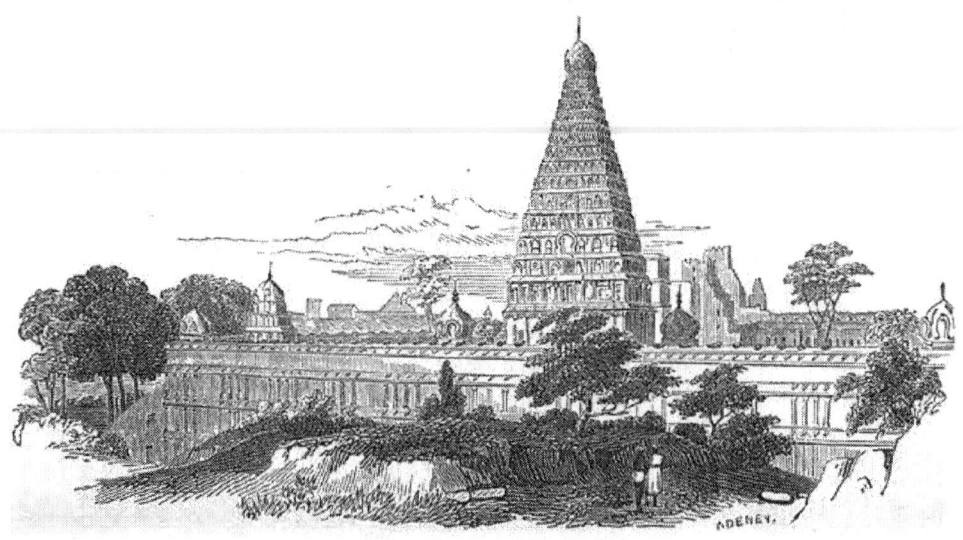

PAGODA AT TANJORE, INDIA.

One of the most bizarre and persistent theories suggests that the **Pharaoh Akhenaten** was actually a human-alien hybrid or a full extraterrestrial, citing his strangely elongated skull, long neck, and spindly limbs as portrayed in Amarna-period art as physical evidence of his non-human origin. Proponents often link this to his radical religious shift toward worshipping the **Aten**—a "sun disk" he claimed to see in the sky—interpreting it not as a star, but as a hovering UFO that provided him with advanced celestial knowledge. While mainstream Egyptologists explain these features as either a specific artistic style or a genetic disorder like Marfan syndrome, the "alien pharaoh" theory remains a cornerstone of the ancient astronaut narrative!

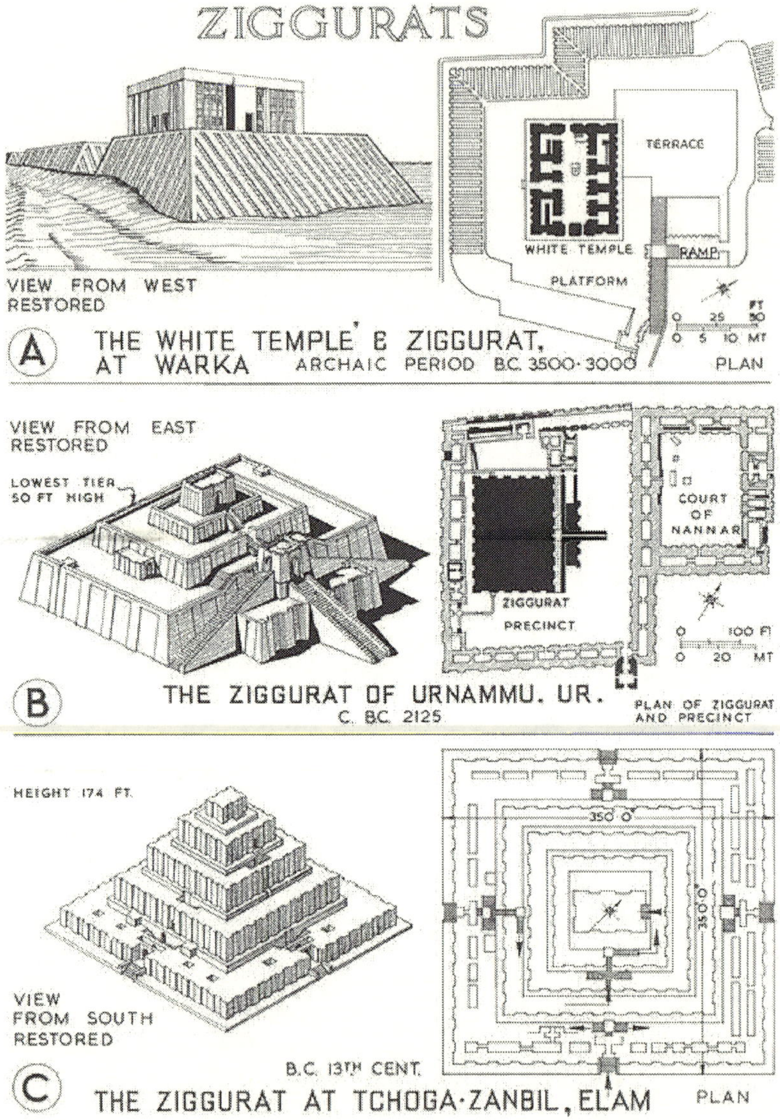

WEST ASIATIC ARCHITECTURE
ZIGGURATS

(A) THE WHITE TEMPLE & ZIGGURAT, AT WARKA ARCHAIC PERIOD B.C. 3500-3000
VIEW FROM WEST RESTORED — PLAN

(B) THE ZIGGURAT OF URNAMMU, UR. C. B.C. 2125
VIEW FROM EAST RESTORED — LOWEST TIER 50 FT HIGH — PLAN OF ZIGGURAT AND PRECINCT

(C) THE ZIGGURAT AT TCHOGA-ZANBIL, ELAM B.C. 13TH CENT.
HEIGHT 174 FT. — VIEW FROM SOUTH RESTORED — PLAN

VIMANAS   ARE   FLYING   CHARIOT   UFOS

Life of Abraham Lincoln - being a biography of his life from his birth to his assassination; also a record of his ancestors, and a collection of anecdotes attributed to Lincoln (1896)

Excerpt: AN OVATION FROM NEIGHBORS, AFTER THE NOMINATING CONVENTION. a mixture of admiration and possibly jealousy; this had not escaped Mr. Lin-coln, and as he shook hands with the judge he inquired, What is your height? Six feet three. What is yours, Mr. Lincoln? Six feet four. Then, said the judge, Pennsylvania bows to Illinois. My dear man, for years my heart has been aching for a president that I could look up to, and Ive found him at last in the land where we thought there were none but littlegiants. The presidential campaign that followed was the most remarkable that hadbeen conducted in the country since the time that William Henry Harrison was ABRAHAM LINCOLN, 137 the Whig candidate for the presidency in 1840, twenty years before. The enthusiasm throughout the North was spontaneous and overwhelming. AbrahamLincoln had come to be regarded as the man of all others to represent the principles and bear the standard of the new party.

Borsippa was an important ancient Sumerian-Akkadian city located about 11-17.7 km southwest of Babylon.

It was considered the "twin city" or "lesser sister-city" of Babylon and a major place of worship for the god Nabu.

The image depicts the ruins of the city's most striking monument, the large ziggurat called the "House of the Seven Lords of Heaven and Earth" (E-urme-imin-anki).

In later Arabic culture, the ziggurat was identified with the biblical Tower of Babel.

The ziggurat was built by King Nebuchadnezzar II (605–562 BCE) and appears to have been destroyed by an extremely hot fire.

This is a coin-operated electric shock machine, likely a **Mills Novelty Company Imperial Shocker**. These were popular in the late 1800s and early 1900s as amusement games and were also advertised as electrical therapy devices.

The machine is a tabletop model with ornate, decorative carvings on its wooden base. The large circular dial features text and a smiling female face in the center, which matches descriptions of the "Take a shock and look pleasant" dial of the Imperial Shocker. One of the two handles is used to control the amount of electrical current delivered to the user. It would have been a 1-cent machine found in saloons and other public places.

The image is a vintage advertisement for Dr. Segonhant's Vapor Bath, a purported disinfectant that claimed to expel disease and poison.

The Strange World of Board Games!!! The history of board games is riddled with oddities that feel more like fiction than fact. For instance, the crossword puzzle was actually banned from New York Public Libraries in the 1920s because librarians feared the "craze" was a waste of time that distracted people from serious research. Similarly, the highest possible scoring word in Scrabble isn't a complex scientific term, but rather "OXYPHENBUTAZONE" (an anti-inflammatory drug), which can theoretically score $1,778$ points if played across three triple-word scores. Even Monopoly has a secret history; during WWII, the British intelligence service smuggled escape maps, compasses, and real currency into POW camps inside special edition Monopoly sets, knowing the Nazis would allow "humanitarian" games to pass through inspection.2. Strange (and True) Finnish Artillery FactsFinland's history with artillery is defined by ingenuity born of necessity.The Musical Mine: During the Continuation War, the Finnish army discovered that Soviet radio-controlled mines were triggered by a specific three-note chord. To jam the signal and prevent explosions, they broadcast the "Säkkijärven polkka" on a loop for months, effectively "drowning out" the trigger frequency with folk music.The Multi-National Arsenal! Due to limited resources, Finland operated the most diverse artillery park in the world, using captured Russian, bought German, French, British, and Swedish guns simultaneously.Sniper Artillery: Finnish gunners were so precise that they often engaged in "direct fire" against individual bunkers and even tanks, treating massive field howitzers like oversized sniper rifles with terrifying accuracy.3. 10 Strange 15th-Century FactsAnimal Trials: It was not uncommon for pigs, rats, or insects to be put on trial for "crimes" like damaging crops or murder, complete with lawyers and judges.The Gutenberg Revolution: Despite changing history, Johannes Gutenberg actually went bankrupt and lost his printing press to his investor, Johann Fust, before he could see his Bible become a massive success. Pointy Shoes (Crakows): Men wore shoes so long and pointy that they sometimes had to be tied to the knees with silver chains just to allow the wearer to walk.The Dancing Plague: In 1491, outbreaks of "dancing mania" occurred where groups of people would dance uncontrollably for days until they collapsed from exhaustion.Mummy Medicine: Europeans began grinding up Egyptian mummies into powder to be eaten as a "cure-all" for various ailments.Sugar Sculptures: At royal banquets, entire scenes (castles, animals, or ships) were carved out of sugar as a display of extreme wealth.The Voynich Manuscript: Created in this century, this book remains written in an entirely undecipherable code that still puzzles linguists today.Coffee Prohibition: When coffee first arrived in some regions, it was briefly banned or treated as a suspicious "Satanic" drink before being blessed by the Pope.Vampire Burial: Graves from this era have been found with bricks wedged into the mouths of the deceased to prevent them from "rising" as vampires.The Printing of Indulgences: One of the first things printed on the new presses wasn't the Bible, but "indulgences"—slips of paper sold by the church to "forgive" sins.4. 9 Weird Yacht FactsThe History of "Yacht": The word comes from the Dutch word jaght, which originally referred to fast pirate-hunting vessels.The Anti-Paparazzi Shield: Roman Abramovich's yacht, Eclipse, features a laser shield designed to detect camera sensors and disrupt them with light to prevent photos.Iceberg Protection: Some "Explorer" yachts are built with reinforced hulls specifically to "ram" through sea ice like icebreakers.The "Gold" Yacht: The History Supreme is rumored to be plated in 100,000kg of gold and platinum, though many experts believe this is an elaborate urban legend.Submarine Hangars: Massive yachts like the Octopus

have internal docks where a full-sized submarine can float right inside the ship.The Floating Hospital: During times of crisis, many of the world's largest yachts are designed to be converted into emergency medical centers.Missile Defense: Several private yachts belonging to billionaires are equipped with military-grade missile detection and decoy systems.The Grass Deck: Some modern yachts feature actual living grass lawns on the upper decks for pets to run on.Support Yachts: Many ultra-wealthy owners have a "shadow yacht"—a second, smaller ship that carries all the "toys" (helicopters, jet skis, cars) so the main yacht stays uncluttered.5. Unknown Facts: Aristotle, Napoleon, & EinsteinAristotleThe First Marine Biologist: He spent years on the island of Lesbos dissecting marine life; he was the first to correctly identify that dolphins are mammals, not fish.The Collector: He was the first person known to have started a systematic library and a "zoo" (a collection of specimens) for research.Hot-Tempered Student: Despite his logic, Plato reportedly called him "the foal," implying he was a young horse that kicks its mother after it has had enough milk.Napoleon BonaparteHe wasn't that short: He was roughly 5'6" or 5'7", which was actually above average for a Frenchman at the time. The "short" myth came from British propaganda.

Romance Novelist: Before he was a general, Napoleon wrote a sentimental romance novella titled Clisson et Eugénie.

Ailurophobia? There is a long-standing myth that he was terrified of cats, but there is actually no historical evidence to support this; it's likely a legend attributed to many "conquerors."

Albert Einstein The Brain Thief: When Einstein died, the pathologist Thomas Harvey stole his brain during the autopsy and kept it in a cider box under a beer cooler for decades to study it.He refused the Presidency: In 1952, Einstein was formally offered the Presidency of Israel. He turned it down, saying he lacked the "aptitude and experience."The Socks Problem: He famously hated wearing socks and stopped wearing them altogether because his big toes would always eventually poke a hole in them.

The image is a woodcut illustration depicting Saint Anthony of Padua preaching to the fish. This event is a popular legend in his hagiography.

Saint Anthony was in Rimini, Italy, where heretics refused to listen to his sermons.

Inspired by God, he went to the mouth of a river and preached to the fish, who miraculously gathered in vast numbers, pushing their heads out of the water to listen.

The people of Rimini, witnessing this miracle, gathered and were moved by his words, leading to their conversion.

The woodcut is an illustration from an old book or incunabula, possibly dating to around 1480.

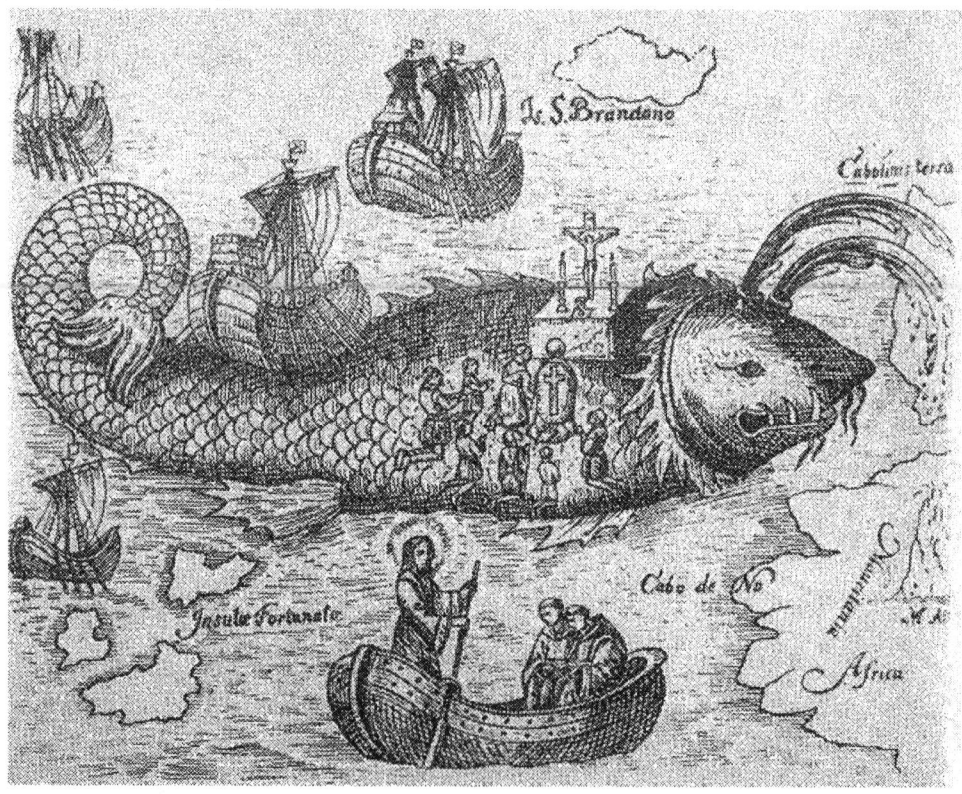

The image provided displays the coat of arms of Geetbets, a municipality located in the Flemish Brabant province of Belgium.

Coat of Arms Details

- The shield is vertically divided into two sections.

- The left section has a green background featuring a silver or white figure of a saint. This figure is St. Gertrude of Nivelles, holding a book and a crozier, with mice associated with her as an attribute.
- The right section has a red background with a bold gold or yellow cross extending to the edges, known in heraldry as a Greek cross or a cross couped.

This design is registered with the Flemish Heraldic Council. The colors and symbols used follow traditional heraldic meanings, with green representing hope and joy, and red symbolizing military strength or a warrior/martyr.

The image displays the coat of arms for the municipality of Boom, Belgium. The shield features the Blessed Virgin Mary with Baby Jesus in front of a tree. Mary is the patron saint of the area. The blue and white colors are traditional colors associated with the Blessed Virgin. She holds a bunch of grapes, symbolizing the historical importance of viticulture in the region.

Saint Scholastica is the patron saint of the Benedictine nuns. She is often depicted with a book and a crozier (pastoral staff). A dove is shown above her head, which, according to legend, is how her soul ascended to heaven.

This specific illustration appears to be used in the coat of arms for the municipality of Alken in Belgium.

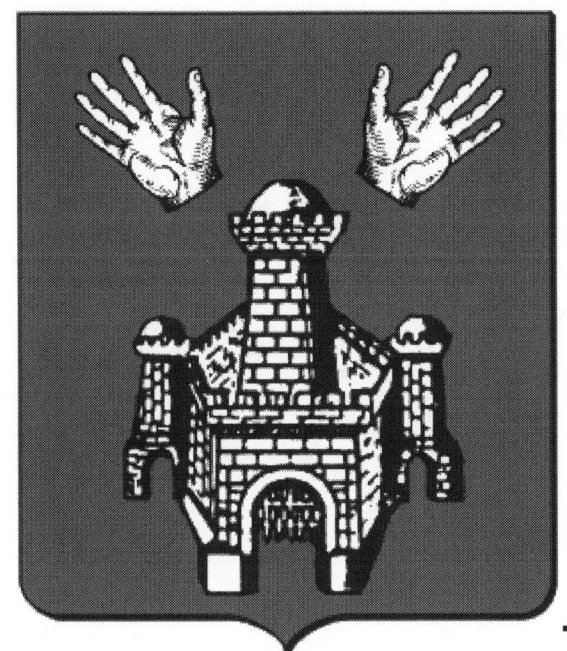

The image displays the coat of arms of the city of Antwerp, Belgium.

The arms depict a castle and two severed hands on a red background.

The imagery is linked to a local folklore about a giant named Antigoon, who demanded a

toll from passing boatmen on the Scheldt river.

According to the legend, anyone who refused to pay had their hand severed and thrown into the river.

A hero named Silvius Brabo eventually killed the giant, cut off his hand, and threw it into the river, which is said to be the origin of the city's name (Dutch: *hand werpen*, "hand-throwing").

BEAUTY IS IN THE EYE OF THE BEERHOLDER.
SCHÖNHEIT LIEGT IM AUGE DES BETRACHTERS.

Made in the USA
Coppell, TX
20 January 2026

68745971R00021